# The Spy's Guide to Undercover Communications

BY
Jim Wiese

WITH
H. Keith Melton
SPY EXPERT

SCHOLASTIC INC.

NEW YORK TORONTO LONDON AUCKLAND SYDNEY
MEXICO CITY NEW DELHI HONG KONG BUENOS AIRES

**Use your red filter to read the message (see page 19)!**

ISBN 0-439-33642-2



Editor: Andrea Menotti
Designers: Robert Rath, Lee Kaplan, Marguerite Oerlemans
Illustrations: Daniel Aycock
Photos: H.K. Melton



12 11 10 6 7/0

Printed in the U.S.A.

First Scholastic printing, December 2002

The publisher has made every effort to ensure that the activities in this book are safe when done as instructed. Children are encouraged to do their spy activities with willing friends and family members and to respect others' right to privacy. Adults should provide guidance and supervision whenever the activity requires.

# TABLE OF Contents

This means you'll use your Spy Gear in this activity.

This means you can find a related activity on the Spy University web site.

# GET the

Okay, spy trainee, time for a little quiz. Which of the following are good places to hide a secret message?

**a. Under a postage stamp.**

**b. On an egg.**

German shepherd puppy needs a good home. Very playful. Has all his shots. Call 469-3480.

**c. In a newspaper ad.**

**d. On a rubber band.**

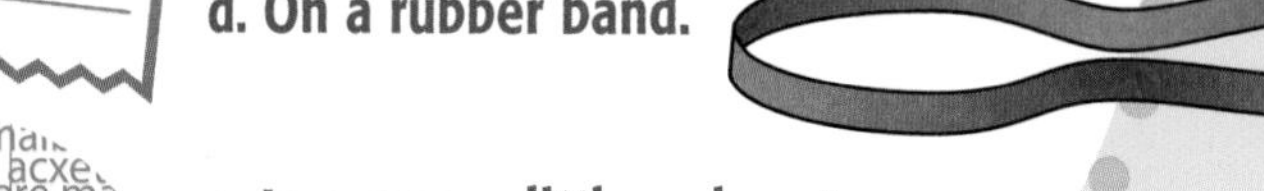

**e. In a messy little red spot.**

**f. All of the above.**

If you picked F, then you're definitely thinking like a spy, and you're all set to take on the tradecraft of undercover communications! This new guide will show you all these ways to hide secret messages and many more.

But undercover communications isn't *just* about hiding your messages. You'll also learn how to arrange secret meetings (so the wrong people won't show up), and how to exchange information using a secret drop-off place called a **dead drop**. (Don't worry—dead drops have nothing to do with dropping dead or anything like that!)

So, let's start by *uncovering* the answers to a few basic questions about spy communication.

# Message OUT!

## Who Do Spies Need to Communicate With?

A spy needs to communicate with his **handler** (the intelligence officer who's in charge of his work). The spy needs to deliver information to the handler, and the handler, in turn, needs to give instructions, equipment, and payment to the spy.

## What's the Best Way for Spies to Communicate?

That's a tough question. Phone conversations can be **tapped**, messages can be intercepted, and a spy can be followed. That's why communication—whether by message or by meeting—is a very big challenge for spies.

Face-to-face meetings are always risky. They can be seen or overheard, and they might attract suspicion if they happen repeatedly, or if one of the people involved is being followed. For these reasons, spies try to avoid personal meetings whenever possible.

Sometimes, to prevent direct contact between members of a **spy network**, a **courier** will deliver secret information from a spy to his handler. Other times, spies will avoid meeting people altogether and use **non-personal contact** to exchange information. That's where dead drops come in.

## What Is a Dead Drop, Exactly?

A dead drop is a secret hiding place where a spy can leave documents, film, or other items for his handler to pick up later. The dead drop system also

**Some examples of dead drop sites. The name "dead drop" probably came about because the drop site is often located inside a "dead" tree stump or an old log.**

works the other way: The handler will use the dead drop to transfer payment and other materials to the spy. In Europe, a dead drop is called a "dead letter box," but it's the same thing–a carefully chosen, well-hidden place for a spy or a handler to leave materials without being seen. It might be a space between two bricks in a wall, a hole in the base of a tree, a hollow space inside an old log, or a hidden spot underneath a small footbridge in a park.

## But How Does the Spy's Handler Know When the Spy Has Placed Materials in the Dead Drop (and Vice Versa)?

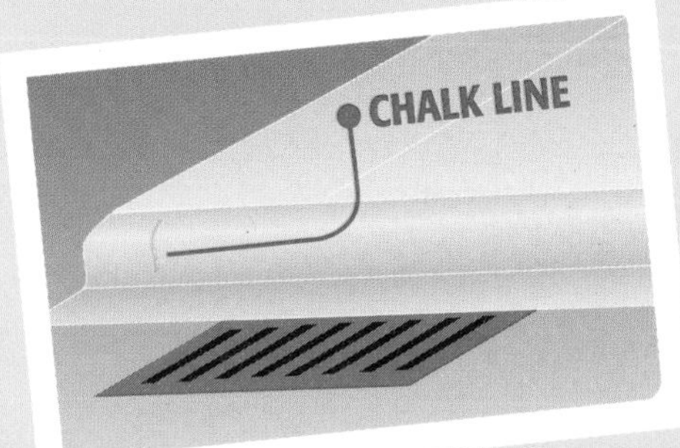


Good question! Here's the answer: The spy will use a **call-out signal** to secretly notify his handler that the dead drop will be filled (or "loaded") at an agreed-upon time. A call-out signal can be as simple as a line of chalk on the side of a curb that the handler walks past every day. When the spy draws the chalk line, the handler will go unload the dead drop at a prescheduled time.

When the handler wants to transfer materials to the spy, the same procedure is followed, except now *the handler* sends the call-out signal and the spy unloads the drop. Usually, a spy and his handler will have many different call-out signals and drop sites. Each call-out signal will be linked to a specific dead drop location.

Call-out signals can also be used as a way to set up meetings. For example, when the chalk line is drawn, that could mean a meeting will occur at noon on the next Tuesday (at a preplanned location).

For all of these types of undercover communication, both the spy and his handler need to plan, learn, and carefully follow procedures. Otherwise, the spy network may find its meetings, messages, and transfers not-so-undercover anymore. So, spy trainee, here's your goal as you head deep into the world of undercover communications: Learn the procedures and stick to them!

**A piece of tape on a sign is a good call-out signal.**

## A word to wise spies

Do these activities with your friends and family in safe places. And don't forget to call in a senior spy when your mission requires one. Be safe, be sure!

## About This Month's Spy Gear

This month, you've been issued the supplies you need to keep your secret messages out of sight. You've got:

- **An invisible ink marker set.** One pen is for writing invisible messages, and the other is for developing the messages later (using a type of chemical called a **reagent**). **Operation Now You See It** on page 10 will show you how it's done.

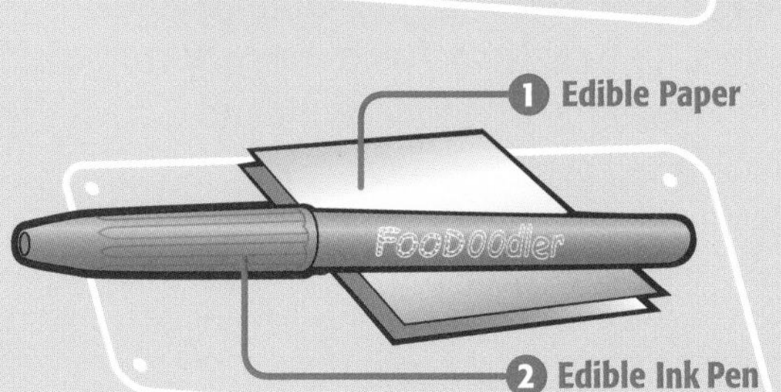


- **Edible paper and an edible ink pen**, so you and your spy network can *eat* your messages after you've read them! That way, the evidence is gone–swallowed without a trace! If that makes your mouth water, check out **Operation Eat Your Words** on page 30.

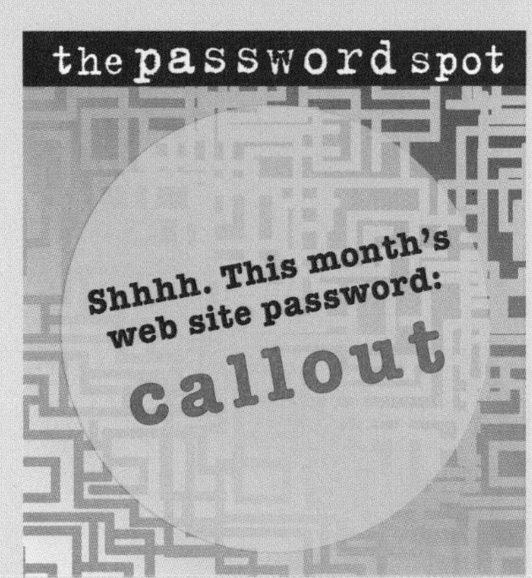


- **Red spy paper, a blue pencil, and a red filter** for color-coded undercover communication. Read all about it in **Operation Red Eye** on page 14.

- **A grille** that you can use to reveal messages in a grid of letters. Turn to **Operation Swiss Cheese** on page 27 to find out how it's done.

## About This Month's Web Site

You'll find a whole new set of training challenges this month on the Spy University web site **(www.scholastic.com/spy)**. You can use a secret writing machine to detect hidden messages, and you can scan scenes for dead drops and call-out signals! So, stop by soon (with your new password, of course!).

**the password spot**

Shhhh. This month's web site password:

callout

# SPY TALK

Here are this month's spy terms. You know the drill: They're shown in **boldface** throughout the book. Learn 'em now, and check back here later if you need a quick review.

▼ **Blind code:** A code that uses newspaper ads and other public messages as secret signals.

▼ **Bona fides:** Good faith, honesty, and sincerity about your identity. When you "establish your bona fides," you prove that you *are* who you *say* you are. (Spies pronounce this BONE-uh-FEE-dees.)

▼ **Call-out signal:** A secret signal that calls someone to a pre-arranged dead drop location or to a meeting.

▼ **Cipher:** A form of code in which the letters of a message are replaced with a new set of letters or numbers according to some rule.

▼ **Code:** A system designed to hide the meaning of a message by using letters, numbers, words, symbols, sounds, or signals to represent the actual text of the message.

▼ **Counterintelligence:** The protection of information, people, and equipment from spies.

▼ **Counterspy:** Someone who works in counterintelligence, investigating and catching spies.

▼ **Courier:** A person who transports materials for an intelligence service.

▼ **Dead drop:** A secret location where a spy or a handler places materials to be picked up later.

▼ **Defector:** A person who leaves the control of a country or intelligence service to serve another country.

▼ **Flash paper:** Paper that burns instantly (to destroy evidence).

▼ **Grille:** A sheet with holes that can be used to reveal a message hidden in a grid of letters.

▼ **Handler:** The intelligence officer who manages a spy's activities.

▼ **Microdot:** A tiny image of a document on film that's so small (less than 1 mm wide), it can only be read with a special magnifier.

▼ **Microwriting:** Writing that's too small to be read by the unaided eye.

▼ **Mole:** An employee of an intelligence service who secretly works for another country's intelligence service.

▼ **Non-personal contact:** Communication that involves dead drops and call-out signals instead of personal meetings.

▼ **Parole:** A special password or phrase that's used to make sure people are who they say they are at a face-to-face meeting.

▼ **Phonetic alphabet:** A system that uses a different word for each letter in the alphabet. (A is Alpha, B is Bravo, and C is Charlie, for example.)

▼ **Reagent:** A chemical used to "develop" invisible ink messages. (Pronounced re-AGE-ent.)

▼ **Scytale:** A round wooden rod that can be used to mask the meaning of messages on thin strips of paper. (Pronounced SIT-uh-LEE.)

▼ **Secret writing:** Techniques used to hide messages.

▼ **Spy network:** A group of spies who work together toward a common goal.

▼ **Steganography:** The art of concealed writing.

▼ **Tap:** To use special electronic devices to listen to and record telephone conversations.

# THE Case OF THE UNKNOWN Sender

It's another day at school, and Ms. Nelson has just asked the class to open their history books to last night's homework assignment. You pick up your textbook, and you're surprised to find a long strip of light blue paper sticking out from between the pages.

You're positive that the strip wasn't there when you did your homework last night. You slowly pull it out, hoping that maybe one of your friends wrote a note on it. But

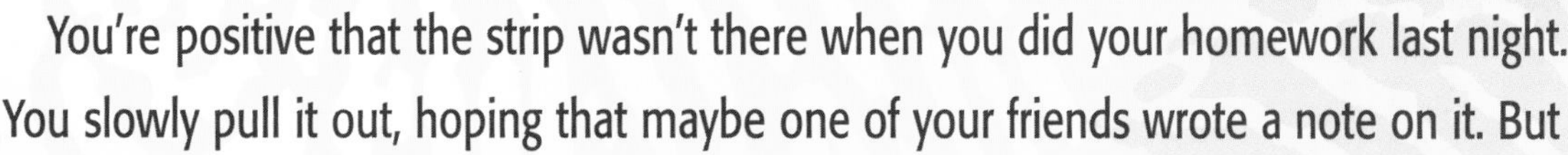

no—it's completely blank. You're about to crumple it up and stuff it in your pocket when you realize that it might be a secret message written in some kind of invisible ink. But which one? You know about lots of invisible inks: lemon juice, milk, invisible ink markers. . . .

If the message was written in milk, you could develop it right now during class, since you've got a pencil with you. But if it was written with an invisible ink marker, you're going to have to wait to develop it, because your friend Liz borrowed your developer marker and promised to give it back at lunch.

- If you think the message might have been written in milk and want to develop it now, turn to **page 13**.
- If you think the message might have been written with an invisible ink marker and want to wait till lunch to use your developer marker, turn to **page 11**.

This is your Spy Quest for this month. There's only one way to solve it, so choose your path wisely! If you hit a dead end, you'll have to back up and choose another path!

#1

OPERATION

# NOW YOU See It

Invisible ink may sound like something out of the world of wizards, but spies have this trick up their sleeves, too. They call it **secret writing**, or "SW" for short. You had a little taste of this in your *Trainee Handbook*, when you learned how to write invisible messages with lemon juice. Now you've got a set of invisible ink markers to make that process a whole lot easier. This operation will show you how to use your new markers to sneak a little something extra onto a regular old postcard!

## Stuff You'll Need

- **Invisible ink marker**
- **Developer marker**
- **Postcard (or plain white paper and envelope)**
- **Pen**
- **Stamp**

## Your Network

- **A friend to receive your message**

## What You Do

**1** Give your friend the developer marker, and let her know to expect an invisible message from you on the bottom of a postcard sometime soon (depending on how fast your mail is!).

**2** Using a regular *visible* ink pen, address the postcard to your friend. Then write a short, innocent note in the message space, maybe something like, "Wish you were here!"

**3** Now, using your invisible ink marker, write your secret message along the bottom of the postcard.

SPYmissions

**4** Put a stamp on the postcard and mail it to your friend. She will reveal the secret writing by running the developer marker over the bottom of the card until the hidden message appears.

(**Note:** If you don't have a postcard handy, you can write your note on plain white paper instead [and mail it in an envelope]. Remember to leave space for your invisible message on the bottom of your note [or on the top, or on the side].)

## More from Headquarters

**1** Switch markers with your friend and have *her* write *you* a hidden message on a postcard!

**2** Instead of telling your friend the general *area* of the postcard where the invisible writing will be, you could put a tiny dot (with your regular pen) where the secret writing starts. To everyone else, it'll look like a simple stray mark, but your friend will know what it means (if you tell her, of course!).

**3** Stop by the Spy University web site at **www.scholastic.com/spy** to use the secret writing machine. See how quickly you can detect hidden messages!

## What's the Secret?

This kind of secret writing works because of a chemical reaction. Both the invisible ink marker and the developer marker (called a **reagent**) contain clear chemicals. But when the chemicals *combine* (when you run the developer over the invisible ink), the new substance is a dark color that you can read.

C
FO
NE
OF
AF
ON
ZY
RQ
NI
EID
UN
AR
FI
TE
TN
XW
PO
IT
EE
TA
ET

*(continued from page 9)*

At lunch, you get your developer marker back from Liz and find an isolated table. As you rub the marker on the strip, a jumble of letters and markings appear, but it's only bits and pieces of writing. You spend a minute or two staring at the strip, and then you realize that it's a scytale! (See page 21 for more on this.)

You wrap the strip around your developer marker, but the letters still don't make sense. You know you have to find a pen or pencil that's just the right size, but the person who made it could have used anything—and lunch is going to end soon. What should you do?

- If you decide to try the scytale on all the pens and pencils that you have right now, turn to **page 36**.
- If you decide to call a meeting of your spy network for some help, turn to **page 33**.

# #2 OPERATION Milky Way

Enough about strong bones and healthy teeth—milk is *more* than just good for you. It's good for **secret writing**, too! You can use milk to write an invisible message that can be developed two different ways. This operation will show you both options so you can choose your favorite. Then, if you're ever stuck without your invisible ink markers, you'll always have the *milky way!*

## Stuff You'll Need

- **Sheet of white paper**
- **Pen**
- **$^1/_4$ cup (65 ml) homogenized whole milk**
- **Cup**
- **Cotton swab**
- **Pencil (for your friend)**
- **Sandpaper (optional—for your friend)**

## Your Network

- **A friend to receive your message**

## What You Do

**1** Using the pen, write a quick friendly note in the center of the paper. Leave lots of space around the note for your invisible message. In this example, we'll use the space below the note, but you can choose any blank area on the paper (as long as you let your friend know where to expect the message).

**2** Pour the milk into the cup.

**3** Dip the cotton swab into the milk and write your secret message along the bottom edge of the page.

**4** Allow the milk message to dry completely. This may take as long as an hour. Don't blot the message or it'll smear. After the milk message has dried, it should be invisible on the white paper.

**5** Pass the note to your friend. To develop the invisible writing, he should scrape a pencil point with sandpaper, letting the pencil dust fall on the message area. (Or, if he doesn't have sandpaper, he can crush the point of the pencil on the corner of the note to get pencil dust.) Then he should use his finger to gently rub the pencil dust over the message area until the words appear.

Hi!
Thanks for your note. It really cheered me up!
-S
Wait for a message from Sam on Tuesday

## More from Headquarters

**1** Remember how lemon juice messages were developed in your *Trainee Handbook*? Well, the same method can be used here. Your friend can reveal the hidden writing by holding the note up to a lamp. He should hold the part of the paper with the invisible writing close to the lightbulb so the paper gets warm. After a few minutes, the message will appear!

**2** Stop by the Spy University web site at **www.scholastic.com/spy**, and see how quick you are at finding and developing secret writing!

## SPYtales

The technical word for hidden or concealed messages is **steganography**. Various forms of steganography (including the use of invisible inks) have been used throughout the world for centuries. As early as the first century C.E., Pliny the Elder explained how the "milk" of the *thithymallus* plant could be used as an invisible ink. Although the milk is transparent after drying, gentle heating cooks the ink, turning it brown.

## What's the Secret?

This invisible ink works because of the substances found in milk. Most of milk is water, but it also contains fat, a food nutrient. The fat in milk is nearly invisible when it's dried on white paper, but when you rub pencil dust over the milk writing, the fat becomes visible. That's because the pencil dust (which is made of graphite, a form of carbon) sticks to the fat in the dried milk and not to the rest of the paper. This makes the writing show up in dark gray (the color of graphite).

If you use heat to reveal the message (as explained in **More from Headquarters**), a chemical reaction occurs. The milk fat contains the element carbon, and the heat will make the carbon visible, turning the writing brown (the color of carbon).

*(continued from page 9)*

It's a good thing you just learned how to reveal a message written in milk! You take a pencil out from your desk and scrape some of the graphite from the point onto the paper. You start rubbing the pencil dust with your fingertip, but the strip remains blank.

Then you hear someone cough behind you. You look up, only to see Ms. Nelson.

"What are you doing?" she asks, frowning.

You're caught off guard and can't think of anything to say on the spot. She sees the blue strip of paper.

"Pay attention, please," she says, taking the paper, tearing it up, and dropping it into the trash.

Not only were you wrong about the milk, but now you've lost the strip of paper!

■ This was a dead end! Turn back to **page 9** and try again!

#3 OPERATION

# REDeye

So far, you've been hiding your messages with invisible inks. But undercover communications can be colorful, too! In fact, you can use the special properties of color and light to hide a secret message right under prying eyes. So, if the thought of snoopers peeking at your secrets makes you see **red**, then this operation is definitely for you!

### Stuff You'll Need

- **Two red filters**
- **Red spy paper**
- **Blue pencil**
- **Red pencil (optional)**

### Your Network

- **A friend to receive your message**

## What You Do

**1** Look carefully at the red box on the left, without using your red filter. What do you notice?

**2** Now, place your red filter on top of the red box. What do you see this time?

**3** Now try making your own color-coded message. Take a sheet of red spy paper and write a message with your blue pencil. Can you see it? If you can, try writing the message more lightly.

**4** If you want to hide your writing even more, you can use a red pencil to add extra letters, or to disguise the letters in your message. For example, you can turn an E into a B, a C into an O, and so on.

SECRET

SECRET

8BORBP

**Use your red filter to reveal the hidden message!**

**5** Give your friend your second red filter at a *different* time from when you send the note. Otherwise, you're giving snoopers all the equipment they need to sneak a peek at your color-coded secrets!

**6** Pass the message to your friend, and she'll use her red filter to read it. Then, if she has her own blue pencil, she can write you back!

## More from Headquarters

**1** If you run out of red spy paper, make more! You just need a red pencil and some white paper (or pink paper). Use shading, letters, symbols, shapes, and designs to make your background as busy as possible. You can even add some light gray pencil marks to mix things up even more!

**2** You can also make more red spy paper on the Spy University web site at **www.scholastic.com/spy**! Be sure to check out the secret writing machine, too—more fun with red filters awaits you there!

## What's the Secret?

To understand why the red filter makes the message show up on the red spy paper, you need to know a little about color and light. White light is a mixture of the seven colors of the rainbow (red, orange, yellow, green, blue, indigo, and violet). When light hits the printing on the page, the red writing reflects only the red part of the light and the blue writing reflects only the blue part of the light.

Now comes the red filter's part. The filter does just what its name says: Because it's a red filter, it *filters* out, or *cancels* out, all of the reflected red light in the image. However, it still lets the blue light get through. So when you look at the red spy paper through the filter, the red printing gets cancelled out, and you can easily see your blue message. (Actually, the blue message looks darker, a kind of purple color, because that's what happens when you mix red and blue colors.)

# #4 OPERATION Egg-citement

News flash: Your lunch bag could contain a secret message! Well, maybe not in your peanut butter and jelly sandwich, but what about that innocent-looking hard-boiled egg? It might look plain and fragile, but an egg definitely has what it takes to hide a secret message (once it teams up with a white crayon and a jar of vinegar!). If that sounds interesting, then you've come to *eggs-actly* the right place!

## Stuff You'll Need

- **Hard-boiled egg**
- **White crayon**
- **Jar with lid (about 16 oz [500 ml])**
- **Vinegar (2 cups [500 ml])**

## Your Network

- **A senior spy (an adult) to make a hard-boiled egg**
- **A friend to receive your egg**

## What You Do

**1** Ask a senior spy to make you a hard-boiled egg. That involves boiling the egg for about ten minutes, rinsing it in cold water, then letting the egg sit in your refrigerator for at least half an hour to cool.

**2** Use the white crayon to write a secret message on the eggshell. Press hard with the crayon, but not so hard that you break the shell! Make sure that each letter in the message is clearly written. You may have to go over each letter a few times. When you're done, the writing should be invisible on the eggshell.

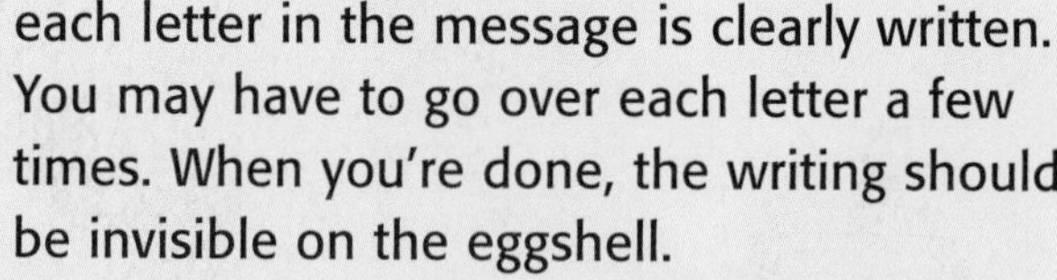

**3** Give the egg to your friend. By following these instructions, your friend can make the writing appear!

**a.** Begin by placing the egg in the jar and adding enough of the vinegar (about 1 cup [250 ml]) to cover the egg.

**b.** Put the lid on the jar. Tiny bubbles should form on the egg. Allow the jar to sit undisturbed for two hours.

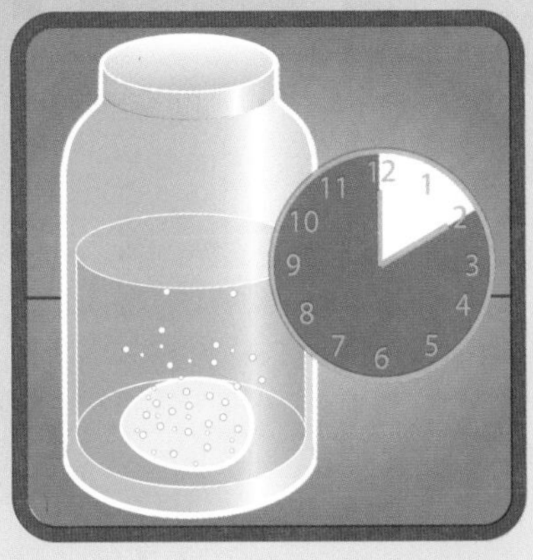

c. After two hours, remove the lid and pour the vinegar out of the jar (without pouring out the egg!).

d. Add another cup of vinegar to the jar, again making sure to cover the egg.

e. After another four hours, dump the vinegar out of the jar and rinse the egg under running water. Gently rub the egg with your fingers as you rinse it. The message should appear!

## More from Headquarters

Stop by the Spy University web site at **www.scholastic.com/spy** and use the secret writing machine for an *eggs-tra* challenge!

## What's the Secret?

The vinegar made the letters appear through a process called *etching*. When your egg takes a bath in vinegar (which is an acid), a chemical reaction occurs, causing the eggshell to dissolve except where it's covered by the wax crayon. This means your crayon letters will stand out, since the shell around them has been etched away!

**P.S.** The etching of the eggshell doesn't affect the egg inside, so your friend can still remove the eggshell (and the evidence of the secret message) and eat the hard-boiled egg inside!

## SPYtales

Non si fanno frittate senza rompere le uova!

Some chemicals can even be used to hide writing *under* an eggshell, on the surface of the hard-boiled egg itself! The process was invented by the Italian scientist Giovanni Porta in the fifteenth century. In Porta's technique, one ounce of alum (a chemical used in dyeing) and a pint of vinegar are mixed together, and then the substance is used to write on the eggshell. The solution soaks through the shell, leaving no trace of the message. But when the eggshell is removed later, the message is printed on the surface of the hardened egg white!

**Above: A message printed under an eggshell, on the surface of a hard-boiled egg! It is in Italian, and it says: "You can't make an omelette without breaking eggs!"**

(continued from page 29)

You run down the hall after Matt. He hears your call and turns around. You ask him why he's here so late after school.

"I'm getting help with my math homework from Ms. Lightly," he replies.

You hold out the paper and ask if it's his.

He shakes his head. "I've never seen that before."

You ask him if he's sure, and he says, "I didn't make that, and I don't know who did. I don't own flowered stationery like that." He gives you a funny look.

"I have to go. Ms. Lightly is waiting for me," he says and walks off.

■ Well, you were wrong. You should've figured that Matt wasn't into flowered stationery to begin with. Turn back and try another path!

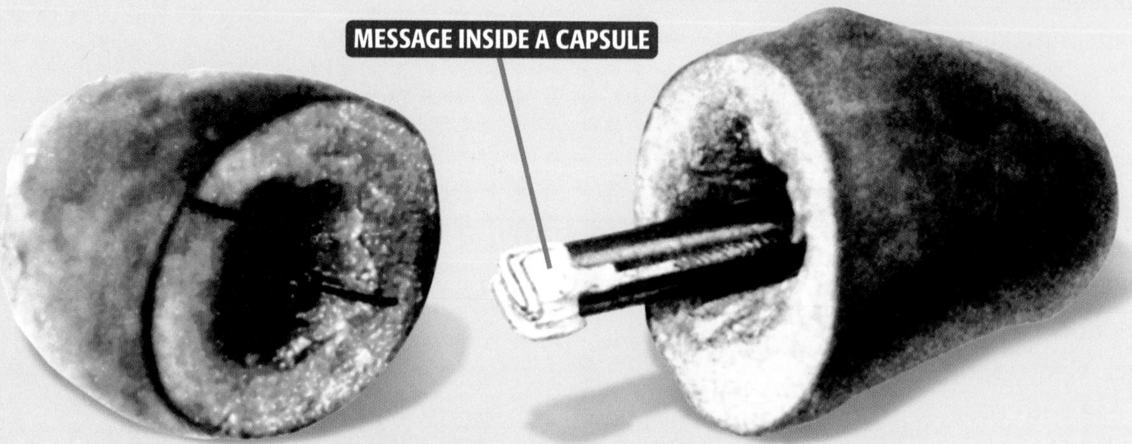


**Eggs aren't the only kind of food that can hide messages. Here's a message hidden inside a hollowed-out potato!**

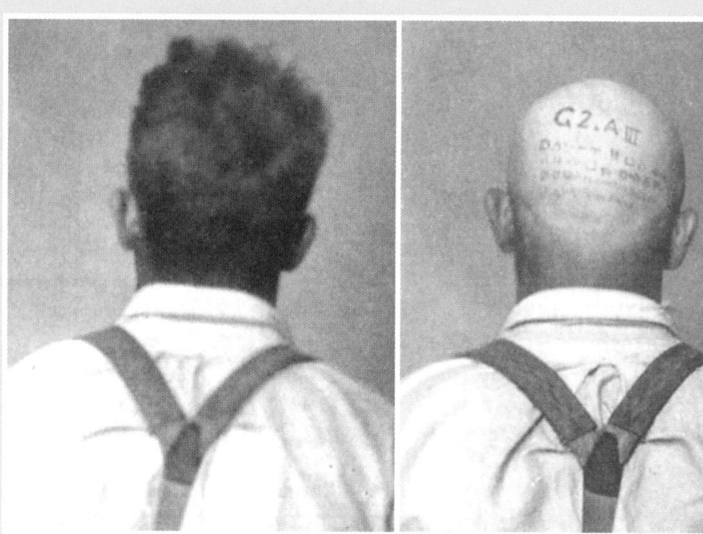

**Hidden messages can even be printed on skin! This Russian spy tried to sneak a message past the Germans during World War I (1914-1918) by having it printed on his bald head and letting his hair grow back over it. Unfortunately, he was caught by German counterintelligence as he traveled across German borders.**

#5

# OPERATION STRETCH It Out

When it comes to sending secret messages, spies have to get creative. They have to think of new and clever ways to use the ordinary items they have around the house. In **Operation Milky Way** and **Operation Egg-citement**, you tried a couple of items from the kitchen—now let's venture over to your desk or supply drawer. Find a thick rubber band, and try this operation to see how it can *expand* into a spy tool!

## Stuff You'll Need

- **Rubber band—at least $^{1}/_{4}$ inch (.5 cm) wide**
- **Book**
- **Ballpoint pen**

## Your Network

- **A friend to receive your message**

## What You Do

**1** Stretch the rubber band as much as possible by placing it around the book.

**2** Use the pen to write a message on the rubber band. Can you read the words clearly?

**3** Take the rubber band off the book. Look at the message when the rubber band is slack. What do you see now?

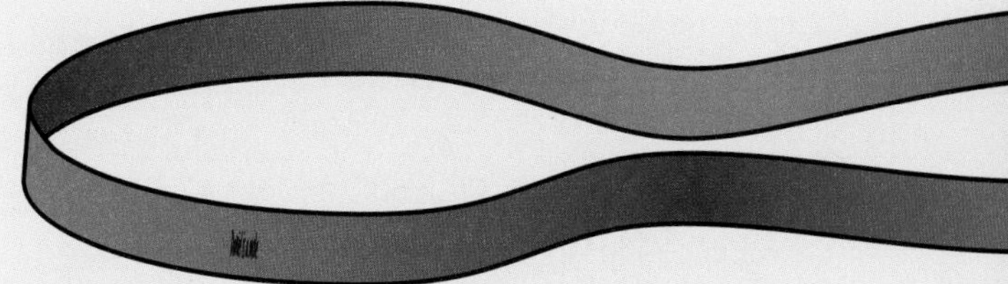

**4** Send the message to your fellow spy by shooting the rubber band at a wall across the room.

**Caution: Never aim a rubber band at a person!**

**5** Your friend can read the message by simply stretching the rubber band so that the words are visible.

## More from Headquarters

Fill a balloon with air and write a message on it with a felt-tip pen. Then let the air out of the balloon. Pass the balloon to your friend. When she blows the balloon up, the message will be clearly visible!

## What's the Secret?

Both the rubber band and the balloon use the stretching properties of rubber to conceal your secret message. When you stretch the rubber band or blow up the balloon, the molecules that make them up are stretched apart. By writing on the stretched rubber, you place the ink on the molecules in a stretched form. When the rubber band is relaxed or the air is let out of the balloon, the molecules move closer together, and the writing ends up looking like a bunch of little lines instead of letters and words. This keeps the message hidden until your friend stretches the rubber band or inflates the balloon!

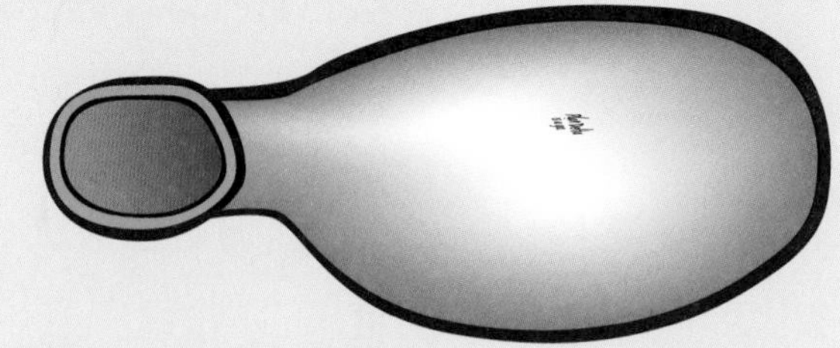

*(continued from page 29)*

You roll up the message with the rubber band and head home. Halfway there, you meet Sarah, another member of your spy network, and show her the new message you've found. The two of you start walking together, trying to figure out what to do with this mysterious grille.

After a while, Sarah starts playing with the rubber band. You keep looking at the paper, until she suddenly stops short. She squints at the rubber band. "There's something weird about this," she says as she hands it to you.

She points to the black, squiggly lines on the rubber band. You stretch it out with your hands and a message appears: MAKE SURE TO RED THE MESSAGE CAREFULLY.

"There's a mistake," Sarah says, after both of you read it. "Red the message? It should be *read* the message. Looks like the secret message writer isn't a very good speller."

A spelling mistake? How strange when the secret message writer was so careful with everything else. You have a nagging feeling that this is more than just a mistake....

"Oh, why didn't I think of it before?" Sarah slaps her forehead. "Do you know Ernie?"

"Oh yeah, he's in my class. He's really good at math."

"Well, he's not so good at spelling. He's always making mistakes like that, and I *know* he's interested in spy stuff. I think Ernie's the one sending the messages!" says Sarah.

Could Ernie be sending you these messages? His house is a block away from yours, so you could stop by on your way home and ask him. But you think that the sender might be giving you a clue. You're almost sure that you could get the clue if you thought about it long enough. What should you do?

- If you decide to go to Ernie's house to ask if he's been sending the messages, turn to **page 22**.
- If you decide to see if the word "red" is a clue, turn to **page 44**.

#6

# OPERATION Wrap IT UP

This mission will take you back in time to the world of ancient Greece, where you'll learn how to use a tool called a **scytale** (pronounced SIT-uh-LEE) to send hidden messages, just like Greek generals from the ancient city of Sparta did. Around 400 B.C.E., Spartan generals used matching scytales (round wooden rods) to write and read secret messages on wound-up strips of parchment. Now it's your turn to create modern-day scytales!

## STUFF YOU'LL NEED

- **Sheet of plain paper (roughly 8½ x 11 inches [22 x 28 cm])**
- **Ruler**
- **Scissors**
- **Tape**
- **Two identical, unsharpened pencils (one for you, and one for your friend)**
- **Pen**

## YOUR NETWORK

- **A friend to receive your message**

## WHAT YOU DO

**1** Use the ruler to measure a half an inch away from the long side of the paper. Draw a line to mark a strip that's ½ inch (1.3 cm) wide and 11 inches (28 cm) long.

**2** Use the scissors to cut the strip from the paper.

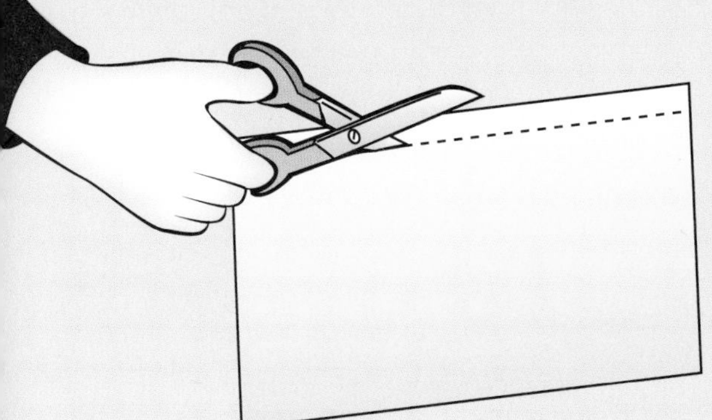

**3** Tape one end of the paper strip to the eraser end of your unsharpened pencil.

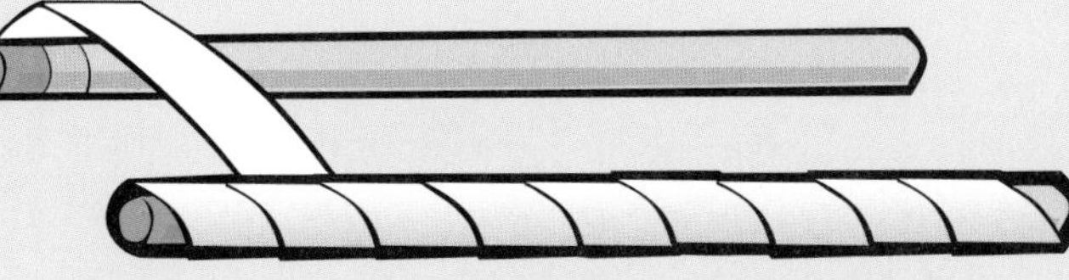

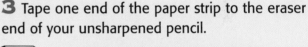

**4** Wrap the paper strip around the pencil in tight spirals so that the top edge of each turn just touches the bottom edge of the previous turn. Tape the other end of the strip to the pencil.



**5** Using your pen, write a secret message in a horizontal line on the wound-up paper. If the message is more than one line long, turn the

(continued from page 20)

You say good-bye to Sarah, and you walk over to Ernie's house, which is on the block just before yours. You knock on the door. His mom answers, and you ask if you can talk to Ernie.

She says, "Oh, I'm sorry, Ernie's been sick this whole week, so he can't come out. Maybe next week." She shuts the door.

That's right—Ernie has been absent from class this whole week! You've been so wrapped up in your search for the sender of the secret messages that you didn't even notice. There's no way, you realize, he could have planted any of those messages. . . .

■ This is a dead end. Turn back and try again!

pencil a little and write another row of words.

**6** Untape the end of the strip and unwrap the paper from the pencil.

**7** Give the strip to your friend. You should also give your friend (at a different time) a pencil to match yours.

**8** Your friend can reveal the secret message by wrapping the strip around the pencil the same way you did.

## More from Headquarters

Now try reading the message using a pencil that's either fatter or thinner than the one you used originally. What happens? Is the message readable?



## SPYtales

The Greeks had other ways of hiding secret messages, too. In 480 B.C.E., Xerxes, emperor of Persia (modern-day Iran), was preparing to invade Greece with a huge army, and he was interested in learning about what sort of men he might encounter. Hearing that the Spartans were the best warriors in Greece, he asked Demaratus, a former Spartan king who was living in Persia, to tell him more. In their conversation, Xerxes told Demaratus of the invasion he'd planned.

At this time, Greeks sometimes wrote on wax that was spread over a wooden tablet. To send his secret message, Demaratus simply wrote a message directly on the wooden tablet, warning the Spartans of Xerxes's plans. He then covered the message with wax, wrote a simple message in the wax, and sent it on.

The message made it safely to Greece, and, given advance warning, the Greeks were able to defeat the Persian army!

Me

**Circumference of pencil**

et

at

my

ho

us

e

af

te

r

## What's the Secret?

For the scytale message to work, both the sender's and the receiver's pencils must have the same circumference. The circumference is the distance around the pencil. If you look at an unwound scytale strip, the spaces between the rows of letters are equal to the circumference of the pencil.

In Sparta, even if messages were intercepted by the enemy, they couldn't be read unless the enemy had a scytale with the right circumference. Otherwise, the letters of the message wouldn't line up properly. Each Spartan general had several scytales with different circumferences. The generals used a **code** at the start of the parchment to tell the reader which scytale to use.

Meet at my house after school. Don't tell anyone else.

Me et oo se ho us n't te e ll te yo r ne

## SPYquest

*(continued from page 33)*

Since you've only got twenty minutes before dinner, everyone immediately begins to examine the strip carefully. The lettering is definitely unreadable, but then Zoe suddenly asks, "Did you look at the back of the strip, too?"

It's worth a shot, so you get out your developer marker and start coloring. Soon a message appears: LOOK UNDER YOUR DESK.

*look under your desk*

The next morning, you get to school early, and Ms. Nelson is the only one in the classroom. You look in your desk, but there doesn't seem to be anything unusual. You slide your hand along the underside of the desk, and your fingers close around an object taped to the bottom. You pull it off. It's candy—a roll of peppermint Life Savers!

At first, you're confused, but then you get it. You're supposed to wrap the scytale around the candy! No wonder none of the regular pens or pencils worked! You take the strip out of your pocket and wrap it around the candy. The message lines up: CHECK FOUNTAIN NEAR MAIN OFFICE AFTER SCHOOL TUES.

a f c r i u n e s
check fountain near main
office after school Tues.
s c h l k z

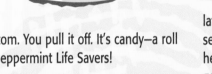

You also notice that the person wrote nonsense letters in the gaps on the strip so you wouldn't be able to guess how to line up the rows of letters. Very clever!

You put the candy in your pocket for later and start thinking. Who could be sending these messages? Whoever it is, he or she obviously has some pretty good spy training. You're tempted to conduct surveillance to catch the person red-handed, but then again, maybe this person is too good to get caught.

- If you decide to just check the main office water fountain after school like the note says, turn to **page 29**.
- If you decide to conduct surveillance on the water fountain and try to catch the sender planting the message, turn to **page 42**.

OPERATION

#7

# STAMP ON IT

Have you ever wanted to look underneath the stamp on an envelope? Most likely not–how could anything of interest possibly fit behind there? But to a spy, the space beneath a stamp is worth checking out. If you thought that writing a secret message on a postcard with invisible ink was sneaky (in **Operation Now You See It**), wait till you try this operation!

## Stuff You'll Need

- **Postage stamp (the lick-and-stick kind)**
- **Postcard**
- **Pencil (well-sharpened)**
- **Small bowl** } **for your friend**
- **Warm water** } **for your friend**
- **Scissors** } **for your friend**

## Your Network

- **A friend to receive your message**

## What You Do

**1** Without licking the back of the postage stamp, lay it on the top-right corner of the postcard where the stamp is supposed to go.

**2** Use the pencil to lightly outline the stamp, making a small rectangle. Remove the stamp. You should now have a small area outlined in the corner that's the same size as the stamp.

**3** Sharpen the pencil as best you can.

**4** Write a short message inside the outline of the stamp.



Make sure to write as small as possible and that none of the writing goes outside the penciled area.

**5** After you've written the message, lick the stamp and stick it in position, covering the message.

37¢
Having a
great time.
Wish you
were here!
V.G. Friend
1 Any Street
Anytown, As
10000


**6** Write a letter to your friend on the left side of the postcard. Keep it short, simple, and unsuspicious!

**7** Then address the postcard to your friend, place it in the mailbox, and wait for it to be delivered. Your secret message has been sent!

**8** Your friend can remove the stamp to reveal the hidden writing by following these steps:

**a.** Fill a small bowl with warm tap water.

**b.** Cut the corner with the stamp off the postcard.

**c.** Place the stamped corner of the postcard in the warm water and let it soak for about five minutes. Soon, the glue on the back of the stamp will dissolve, and the stamp will start floating off the paper!

**d.** Remove the corner of the postcard from the water, pat it dry (don't rub!), and read the message!

(**Note:** If you don't want to destroy the postcard, you don't have to cut the corner off. You can just dip the stamped corner of the postcard into the water.)

## More from Headquarters

Visit the Spy University web site at **www.scholastic.com/spy** to use an x-ray detector to reveal hidden writing underneath stamps (and more!).

## What's the Secret?

In this operation, you wrote your message as small as possible so it would fit under a postage stamp. Spies have used miniature writing, called **microwriting**, as a method for sending secret messages for years. During World War I (1914–1918), a French spy named Paul Bernard wrote a 1,600-word report in the space beneath a postage stamp! He used shorthand (a special writing method that involves abbreviations and symbols) to condense the report.

Nowadays, spies don't have to rely on handwriting skills like that. They can easily shrink whole messages (or any document) to the size of a tiny dot! These dots are called **microdots**, and they're made by photographing a document with a special microdot camera. The camera reduces the document to a 1-mm (or smaller) dot on a piece of film. The tiny piece of film

**These postage stamps provided a way to hide this sketch of a torpedo so it could be mailed to a Russian spy working in Germany during World War I (1914–1918). The sketch was discovered by German counter-intelligence officials who were closely examining all mail sent to the spy's address.**

can then be placed under a stamp, tucked into a slit that's been cut in the edge of a postcard, or hidden in any secret compartment (like in a ring or a fake coin). Once received, the microdot can be read using a special magnifier.

## SPYtales

During the American Civil War (1861–1865), spies working for the Confederate Army were already using an early form of microdot technology. The agents shrank their messages by taking pictures of them, and then they hid the miniature photos inside hollow buttons sewed onto their coats. This way, the agents could walk across enemy lines carrying a lot of valuable information in a secure way.

**A microdot (actual size and enlarged).**

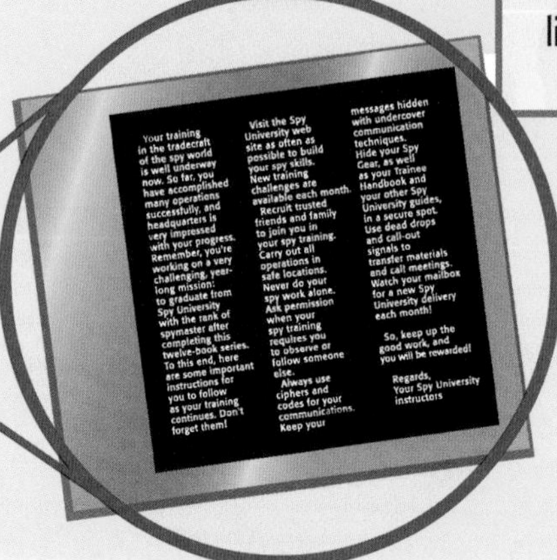

Your training in the tradecraft of the spy world is well underway now. So far, you have accomplished many operations successfully, and headquarters is very impressed with your progress. Remember, you're working on a very challenging, year-long mission: to graduate from Spy University with the rank of spymaster after completing this twelve-book series. To this end, here are some important instructions for you to follow as your training continues. Don't forget them!

Visit the Spy University web site as often as possible to build your spy skills. New training challenges are available each month.

Recruit trusted friends and family to join you in your spy training. Carry out all operations in safe locations. Never do your spy work alone. Ask permission when your spy training requires you to observe or follow someone else.

Always use ciphers and codes for your communications. Keep your messages hidden with undercover communication techniques. Hide your Spy Gear, as well as your Trainee Handbook and your other Spy University guides, in a secure spot. Use dead drops and call-out signals to transfer materials and call meetings. Watch your mailbox for a new Spy University delivery each month!

So, keep up the good work, and you will be rewarded!

Regards,
Your Spy University instructors

**A tiny camera, shown actual size, used by East German agents to make microdots.**

**This microdot viewer magnifies microdots so they can be read. The microdot is placed against the glass slide, and the magnifier is inserted into the holder. Then the entire device is held up to a light so the microdot can be read.**

## SPYquest

*(continued from page 33)*

Your spy network decides to tail Matt at school the next day. Tailing duty is divided up, and you're assigned to tail Matt before school starts.

You get to school early and keep an eye out for Matt. Finally, he comes down the hallway, and you pretend to do something else to see if he tries to deliver another message. You watch carefully, but Matt just sits at his desk and starts doodling in his notebook.

You meet with your spy network that afternoon to share results, and everyone agrees that Matt isn't the one dropping off the messages. No leads here.

■ This is a dead end. Turn back and try again!

#8

# OPERATION SWISS Cheese

In your Spy Gear kit this month, you'll find two yellow cards with lots of holes punched in them. They might look a little Swiss-cheesy, but really they're great message-hiding tools. They're called **grilles**, and you can use them to hide a message in a big crowd of letters. Read on, and you'll get the *hole* idea!

## STUFF YOU'LL NEED

- **Two grilles**
- **Paper**
- **Paper clip**
- **Scissors**
- **Pencil**

## YOUR NETWORK

- **A friend to receive your message**

## GRILLE IT UP!

| A | J | D | M | L | R | I | C | K | O | Q | Z | T | H | P | V | N | U |
|---|---|---|---|---|---|---|---|---|---|---|---|---|---|---|---|---|---|
| F | S | P | W | X | B | O | R | W | A | S | K | M | U | F | T | L | I |
| Z | V | Y | K | E | J | T | L | C | E | Q | V | U | T | O | A | D | Z |
| J | U | R | P | J | B | Q | M | R | Y | E | O | K | D | Q | T | W | Y |
| I | Y | H | Z | H | A | M | S | U | B | X | D | E | P | T | I | B | L |
| K | Q | U | O | D | D | T | I | P | F | Z | G | J | I | L | P | E | S |
| H | E | C | T | G | H | S | U | E | I | C | F | Q | N | C | L | U | Y |
| X | R | H | G | S | T | W | X | M | L | R | C | S | G | T | G | X | I |
| M | T | L | M | A | T | F | S | O | D | T | H | D | N | V | O | P | L |
| W | A | O | T | Z | D | Q | X | Y | E | A | J | O | M | L | Q | X | R |
| L | F | U | I | T | H | G | D | F | B | H | N | U | K | W | S | T | P |
| V | Y | E | F | Q | G | T | E | C | T | V | W | A | U | S | I | Z | X |

**Can you use your grille to find the message hidden here?**
**You can check your answer on page 48.**

## What You Do

### Part 1: Reveal a Message

**1** Look at the grid of letters on the previous page. It looks like a word search, but it actually contains a secret message.

**2** To read the hidden message, place your grille over the grid of letters (with the Spy Gear eyes facing up). Read the letters from left to right, starting at the top of the grille and working your way down.

### Part 2: Create a Message

**1** To write your own secret message, place your grille on a sheet of blank paper (with the Spy Gear eyes facing up). Use a paper clip to hold the grille in place.

**2** Use the scissors to cut the paper so it's exactly the same size as the grille.

**3** Write the letters of your message through the windows of the grille onto the white paper. Write the letters the same way you read–from left to right, and from top to bottom.

**4** If your message is long, you can use a second sheet of paper to fill in the rest of the letters.

**5** Remove the paper clip and separate the grille and paper. Write other letters in the blank spaces around the letters of your message, so that the message is completely hidden.

**6** Give your friend the second grille sometime *before* you pass the message.

**7** Pass the message. Your friend will place the grille over it and read the letters from left to right, starting at the top and moving to the bottom.

## More from Headquarters

Create your own grilles! Using scissors and cardboard, you can create grilles with larger windows so that whole words can fit inside them. Then the grilles can be placed over innocent-sounding notes to reveal secret messages lurking within the words!

## What's the Secret?

In this hidden writing technique, only someone who has a matching grille can read your message. Without the grille, the message is just a jumble of letters. Good luck to anyone who tries to *find a word* in there!

**Here's one more hidden message for you! Use your grille to find it!**

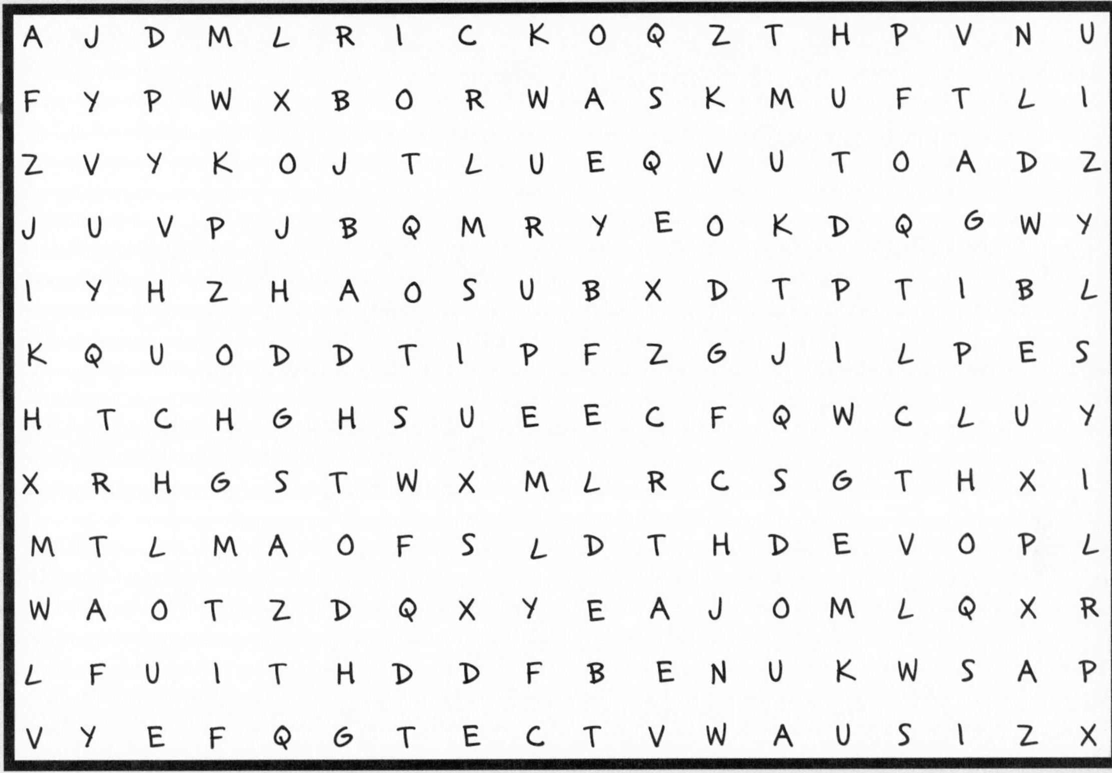

| A | J | D | M | L | R | I | C | K | O | Q | Z | T | H | P | V | N | U |
|---|---|---|---|---|---|---|---|---|---|---|---|---|---|---|---|---|---|
| F | Y | P | W | X | B | O | R | W | A | S | K | M | U | F | T | L | I |
| Z | V | Y | K | O | J | T | L | U | E | Q | V | U | T | O | A | D | Z |
| J | U | V | P | J | B | Q | M | R | Y | E | O | K | D | Q | G | W | Y |
| I | Y | H | Z | H | A | O | S | U | B | X | D | T | P | T | I | B | L |
| K | Q | U | O | D | D | T | I | P | F | Z | G | J | I | L | P | E | S |
| H | T | C | H | G | H | S | U | E | E | C | F | Q | W | C | L | U | Y |
| X | R | H | G | S | T | W | X | M | L | R | C | S | G | T | H | X | I |
| M | T | L | M | A | O | F | S | L | D | T | H | D | E | V | O | P | L |
| W | A | O | T | Z | D | Q | X | Y | E | A | J | O | M | L | Q | X | R |
| L | F | U | I | T | H | D | D | F | B | E | N | U | K | W | S | A | P |
| V | Y | E | F | Q | G | T | E | C | T | V | W | A | U | S | I | Z | X |

*(continued from page 23)*

After class is dismissed, you wait till everyone leaves and head over to the water fountain near the main office. After you make sure no one's watching, you look under the fountain.

Aside from wads of gum (gross!), you see a rolled up piece of paper with a rubber band around it, wedged in between the pipes. You pull the paper out and open it up.

It's a blank piece of flowered stationery that seems ordinary, except for one thing–it has tiny squares cut out of it in random places. You suspect it's a grille

and examine the front and back to see if there are any more clues. There's nothing you can see.

Suddenly, out of the corner of your eye, you see Matt walking down the hallway. What's Matt doing here after school? You still suspect that he might be the one sending the messages, and the fact that he's still here is suspicious.

But then you look back at the piece of stationery you just received, and you know there must be something you've missed. . . .

■ If you decide to confront Matt directly, turn to **page 18**.

■ If you decide to examine the message further, turn to **page 20**.

# OPERATION Eat YOUR WORDS

So far, you've learned lots of ways to keep your secret messages undercover as they change hands. But what do you do with a message *after* you've read it? If you throw it in the trash, someone could dig it out and read it. If you keep it, you could get caught holding evidence against you! Spies have many ways to get rid of secret messages after they've read them, but some methods are tastier than others—and the method you'll learn in this operation is the tastiest of all! So, if you think your secrets are good enough to eat, open wide. . . .

## STUFF YOU'LL NEED

- **Edible paper**
- **Edible ink pen**

## YOUR NETWORK

- **A friend to receive your message**

## WHAT YOU DO

### PART 1: TRY IT, YOU'LL LIKE IT!

This set of pen and paper isn't like the pen and paper you use to do your homework. The ink and the paper are *edible*, which means you can eat your notes! Before you start sending messages, have a little taste test to see what you're working with.

**1** Write a few words on a piece of edible paper with the edible ink pen.

**2** Tear a small piece off the paper and stick it in your mouth. What happens?

**3** Try eating a larger piece of paper. How does it taste? Can you figure out what flavor it is?

**4** Try all the different paper colors. Can you identify each flavor? You can check page 48 to see how accurate your taste buds are!

### PART 2: THE EDIBLE MESSAGE

Now that you know how your edible paper tastes, try using it to send a message.

Be careful.
Molly cannot
be trusted.

**1** Use the edible ink pen to write a message on a piece of edible paper. You'll notice that one side of the paper is smoother than the other and easier to write on. The other side can be used if your message is too long to fit on one side.

**2** Carefully fold the paper in half several times to cover the writing and make the note smaller.

**3** Pass the note to your friend. To keep it undercover, tuck it inside a book and pass it to her that way. Or, since it's edible, you could even stash it inside her lunch bag!

**4** Once your friend reads the note, she can destroy it by simply popping it in her mouth and eating it!

**Caution:** Don't eat edible paper that has been written on with other (non-edible) inks.

## More from Headquarters

**1** To keep your message even safer, write it in a **code** or **cipher**. Consider using the Caesar cipher you learned in your *Trainee Handbook*.

**2** Skip ahead to **Operation Dead Drop** on page 34, and try passing your edible message using a dead drop!

## What's the Secret?

Your edible paper and ink are great for secret messages because you'll be able to quickly destroy the evidence of your spy communications by eating them!

Most paper is made from wood products, which *are* actually edible, but you wouldn't *want* to eat them. While some animals can eat wood products, it's hard for people to chew and digest them. That's why your edible paper is actually made from food—it's a mixture of potato starch, water, vegetable oil, artificial flavoring, and food coloring. This mixture is rolled out and cooked so it becomes like a very thin potato pancake. The paper can be made in different flavors and colors, depending on the type of flavoring and coloring added to the mixture.

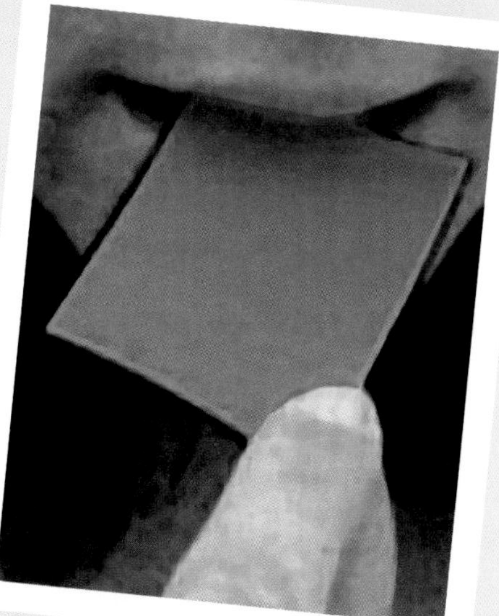

Most inks are made from dyes that aren't good for you to eat. But your edible ink pen uses ink made from food coloring. When you use it to write on edible paper, there's no problem with swallowing the evidence!

Edible paper is one way to make sure that a secret message isn't discovered after it's been read. But spies have other ways to quickly destroy a message if **counter-spies** are hot on their trail. One way is to use **flash paper**. Normal paper will burn, but it takes a while for it to burn completely. In some cases, even after the paper is burned, it's still possible to read what was written on it. Flash paper contains chemicals that are highly *flammable* (they catch fire very easily). These chemicals make the paper burn almost instantly, leaving very little ash behind. If counterspies are about to close in, the spy will put a match to the paper, and in the blink of an eye, the paper, along with its secret message, will be gone!

**Flash paper burns very fast!**

OPERATION

# #10 CALL OUT

It's risky when a spy talks directly to a member of his spy network. Every time they make direct contact, there's a chance that they're being watched by **counter-spies**. To avoid direct contact, spies and their networks can use a series of **call-out signals** and **dead drops** to pass information back and forth. A call-out signal is a way to let a member of a spy network know that a dead drop will be loaded or that a meeting needs to happen. You'll learn more about dead drops in your next mission, **Operation Dead Drop**. But first, here's a quick introduction to call-out signals.

### Stuff You'll Need

- **Masking tape**

### Your Network

- **A friend to *call out* to a meeting**

## What You Do

**1** The first step is to work with your friend to decide on a call-out signal that you'll use to set up meetings. For example, the signal site may be a road sign that you and your friend walk by every day. The call-out signal could be a 1-inch (2.5 cm) piece of tape placed at a certain place on the sign. Every day, you and your friend will check the sign, looking for the call-out signal.

**2** Give this call-out signal a code name, like *Call-Out Orange* or *Call-Out Maple Leaf*. Choose any code name you want, but make sure the name has nothing to do with the location of the signal. This is a security precaution, in case the code name is overheard by people outside of your spy network. You wouldn't want them to know where to look for your signal!

**3** Next, decide when and where you'll meet each time you see the call-out signal. For example, you may want to meet at your house at noon on the first Saturday after the signal is posted.

**4** When you need to meet your friend, put the 1-inch (2.5-cm) piece of tape on the sign.

**5** When your friend sees the tape, he knows that he should meet you the next Saturday at noon at your house, just like you arranged.

**6** Your friend will remove the tape as a signal back to you that he has seen the signal and will be at the meeting.

## More from Headquarters

**1** Your call-out signal could be as simple as having the shade in your window pulled down halfway, having a flowerpot appear in your windowsill, or even wearing a shirt of an unusual color on a certain day. As long as your friend walks by your house every day (and checks your window), or sees you daily in school, this will work just fine.

**2** Visit the Spy University web site at **www.scholastic.com/spy** and scan some scenes for hidden call-out signals. See how quickly you can spot them!

## What's the Secret?

A call-out signal is another form of **code**. Remember, a code can be any symbol (like a piece of tape or a line of chalk) that's given special meaning by a certain group of people. The key is that only the *insiders* know what it means, while *outsiders* don't.

*(continued from page 11)*

You decide to call a meeting of your spy network, Spy Force One. Since everyone walks by your house on the way home from school, the call-out signal is a piece of tape on the stop sign on your corner. This means that there's a meeting at 4:00. You run home ahead of everyone and put the tape on the sign.

At 4:00, everyone shows up, and you explain what's happened. You show everyone the piece of paper and say that you think it's a scytale.

Liz says, "Well, why don't we all get out our pens and pencils and try to see if one of them works?"

Everyone agrees and starts looking through their bags. Twenty minutes later, there's a pile of pens and pencils on your bedroom floor, but even so, the message is still a mystery.

"I can't believe it," says Jeff. "There must have been fifty pens or pencils between the six of us, but none of them worked! We even tried using our fingers, but nothing made the message make sense!"

"Hmmm," says Zoe, studying the paper. "Scytales usually have blank spaces between the letters, but this seems to hardly have any spaces at all. We probably should keep checking the strip for clues."

"I think it would be faster if we try to find out who the sender is," says Sam. He turns to you. "Do you know anyone who might have sent it?"

C
FO
NE
OF
AF
ON
ZY
RQ
NI
EID
UN
AR
FI
TE

You try to think of anyone who could have possibly put the message on your desk, and you remember that your friend Matt sits next to you in class. He could have slipped the strip in your book when you weren't looking. You mention this to the others.

"I think we should tail Matt at school tomorrow to see if he's dropping off messages," says Sarah.

It's almost dinnertime, so you've got to make a decision.

- If you decide to have your spy network follow Matt around school tomorrow, turn to **page 26**.
- If you decide to examine the strip again, turn to **page 23**.

# #11 OPERATION Dead DROP

A **dead drop** definitely isn't *deadly*—in fact, it's a very *safe* way for a spy to pass materials to his **handler** (and vice versa), since it doesn't require any personal contact. In a dead drop operation, a spy places his materials (documents, film, or whatever else) in a carefully chosen secret location, and his handler picks them up later. The dead drop can also work for the handler. He can use the *reverse* procedure to leave money or supplies for the spy. Try this activity to learn more about how to choose and use a dead drop.

### Stuff You'll Need

- **Pencil and paper**
- **Small plastic bag to hold your message (optional)**
- **Chalk**
- **Masking tape**

### Your Network

- **A friend to pick up your message**

## What You Do

**1** Pick out a good site for your dead drop. Dead drops are usually outside, so go out and explore. Choose a place where people are normally seen and you'd normally go, but—here's the trick—find a spot that's a little hidden away, so your materials won't be visible to anyone who happens to be walking by. This might be the space beside a broken brick in a wall, inside the hollow of a tree, or on the ground underneath a rock. Keep in mind that this spot has to be easy to identify and

describe to someone else. Also try to find a spot that you can load easily and quickly without being seen. Once you've found a single place that meets all of these requirements (hint: parks and gardens are good bets), you're all set to move on to step 2.

**2** Give the dead drop a name, like *Dead Drop Rose* or *Dead Drop Eagle*. The name should have nothing to do with the dead drop's location, because you don't want the name to give a **counterspy** any hints, should he happen to hear about it. So don't call your location *Dead Drop Playground* if that's where it is!

**3** Explain to your friend where the dead drop is located. Draw a map if necessary.

**4** You and your friend should also agree on a **call-out signal** that will let your friend know that you're about to load the dead drop. Turn back to **Operation Call Out** (on page 32) for specific instructions on how to choose a call-out signal site. For this example, we'll use a line of chalk on the side of a curb that you and your friend walk past each day. When your friend sees this chalk line, she'll know to go unload the drop at an agreed-upon time (like the next evening, for example).

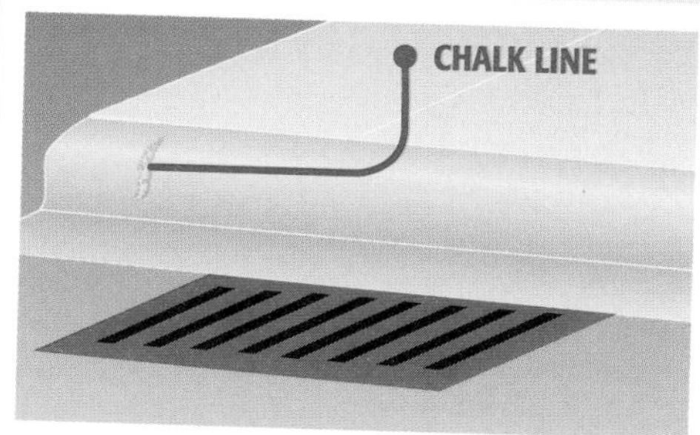


**5** Write a short message to your friend using the pencil and paper.

**6** If you think it might be rainy, or if your dead drop is at all moist, then put your message inside a plastic bag (or another container).

**7** Use your call-out signal (the line of chalk) to let your friend know that you're going to load the dead drop.

**8** Casually go to the dead drop site, and when you're sure no one's looking, place the message inside.

**9** Having seen your signal, your friend will go to the dead drop site and pick up the message at the time you arranged. To make sure this goes off without a hitch, you can leave another signal (like your call-out signal) right after you load the drop. This could be a piece of tape on a sign near the drop site. When your friend unloads the drop, she'll remove the tape to let you know that the message was received.

## More from Headquarters

**1** Try setting up dead drops in some of these locations:

- Put the message inside a particular book in your local library (or your school library). Try to choose an unpopular book, and make sure the drop is unloaded quickly (in case some-one decides to give your book a chance!).

Dead drops can also be placed into the ground using containers like this one, called a "dead drop spike."

- Roll the message into a tight cylinder, then tie a string to it. Hide the message between two bricks or rocks and leave the string exposed. The string can be used to pull the message out of its hiding place.

- Sit on a park bench and casually stick the message beneath the bench seat (using a tape loop or a thumbtack) for pickup by a member of your **spy network**.

- Try to locate a good dead drop location in your school. Although most dead drops are located outside, they can also be *inside*. Public restrooms are popular places for drop sites.

**2** How sharp are your eyes? Stop by the Spy University web site **www.scholastic.com/spy** and see if you can identify dead drops by scanning a scene!

## What's the Secret?

Here are the main factors spies consider when they're choosing their dead drop sites.

- The spy has a good reason to be in the area and won't attract attention.
- The spy has quick access to the site and a way to exit quickly.
- The location is private enough that the drop can be loaded and unloaded secretly.
- The drop won't be seen or disturbed by outsiders.
- The location is easy to find and describe to other members of your spy network.

*(continued from page 11)*

You rummage through your bag and dump all of your pens and pencils out onto the cafeteria table. You try winding the strip around each of them, but no luck. The message is still gibberish. If only you knew which pen or pencil was the right size!

■ This is a dead end! Go back and try again!

# John Walker

## An American Who Spied for the Soviet Union

American John Walker was a spy for the former Soviet Union from 1967 to 1985. For years, he delivered U.S. Navy secrets to the KGB (the intelligence service of the former Soviet Union). Walker and his KGB handlers used an elaborate system of dead drops and call-out signals to transfer secret information and payments.

First, KGB officers placed an empty 7-Up can upright on the edge of the road at an agreed-upon spot. This signaled to Walker that the KGB was ready to make an exchange. The next move was up to him. Five miles beyond the KGB's signal site, Walker would put another 7-Up can upright beneath a roadside telephone pole. He then would continue to the dead drop location, where he would leave his bundle of secret documents behind another telephone pole.

While Walker was dropping off his package, the KGB would leave a package of cash for him in a spot a few miles away. Then, the KGB handlers would leave Walker *another* can to indicate that they'd retrieved the package of information, and Walker would leave a final can at yet *another* location to indicate that he'd received the money.

This activity continued for almost twenty years. During that time, Walker gave away countless secrets of the U.S. Navy, including the movements of its nuclear submarine fleet. Finally, Walker's ex-wife informed the FBI of his activities and he was caught, tried, and sentenced to life in prison.

**John Walker, following his arrest, is shown demonstrating how he used his Minox camera to photograph documents.**

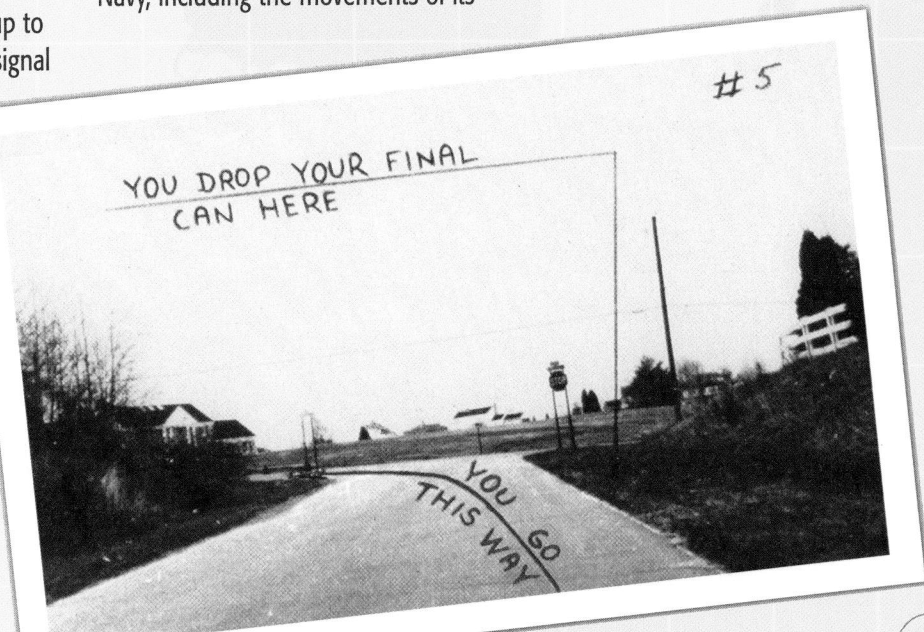


**The KGB provided this photograph with written instructions on it to explain to Walker where to leave his final signal can.**

# #12 OPERATION LETTER Lingo

If anyone's ever spelled a word for you over the phone, you know how hard it is sometimes to tell the letters apart. The letters B and P, for example, can sound very much alike. Spies have the same problem when they're receiving communications by phone or by radio. To avoid confusion, they'll use the **phonetic alphabet**.

**Stuff You'll Need**

- **Pencil and paper**
- **Telephone**

**Your Network**

- **A friend to help you test the phonetic alphabet on the phone**

**The word "phonetic" means "relating to spoken language."**

The phonetic alphabet assigns a special word to each letter of the alphabet (so B is Bravo and P is Papa, for example). This special alphabet was adopted in 1957 for use all over the world. It's a very handy system for communications, and also for giving code names to agents and **dead drop** locations. So, try this operation to learn your ABCs all over again—this time as Alpha, Bravo, and Charlie!

A - Alpha
B - Bravo
C - Charlie
D - Delta
E - Echo
F - Foxtrot
G - Golf
H - Hotel
I - India
J - Juliet
K - Kilo (KEE-lo)
L - Lima (LEE-ma)
M - Mike
N - November
O - Oscar
P - Papa
Q - Quebec (Qua-BECK)
R - Romeo
S - Sierra
T - Tango
U - Uniform
V - Victor
W - Whiskey
X - X-ray
Y - Yankee
Z - Zulu

## What You Do

**1** Learn the phonetic alphabet. Each letter is represented by a word, so say the words to yourself (in order) until you can remember them.

**2** Test out the phonetic alphabet by saying some groups of letters to your friend over the phone. Try these three: MSV, PTN, FDB. Speak quickly, and have your friend write the letters down as you say them. Don't repeat anything, even if your friend asks!

**3** Now say the same letter groups again, but in phonetic alphabet words. Say: Mike Sierra Victor, Papa Tango November, and Foxtrot Delta Bravo. Have your friend write down the letter each word represents.

**4** Ask your friend to compare the first list of letters with the second. Did the letters come across more easily the second time? That's the idea!

## More from Headquarters

**1** Use the phonetic alphabet to create a code name for each member of your **spy network**. For example, you might be known as FX1 (Foxtrot X-ray One). This will help keep your real identity a secret when you communicate.

**2** Use the phonetic alphabet to name your dead drop sites. You could have names like Dead Drop Alpha, Dead Drop Zulu, Dead Drop Romeo Juliet, or anything you want! Do the same for your call-out signal sites.

## What's the Secret?

The phonetic alphabet uses words that are common in many different languages. This prevents confusion between similar-sounding letters, and it helps clarify communications that may be garbled in transmission. The phonetic alphabet is used by the military, by airplane pilots communicating with control towers, by CB (citizen band) and short wave radio operators, and even by astronauts flying in space!

## More Spy Conversation Tips

**1 Use a time code** If you decide to set up a meeting over the phone and you're concerned you may be overheard, use a special time code. When stating the time of the meeting, you and your spy network can agree that you will add a certain number of hours to the actual meeting time (or you could choose to subtract the hours). For example, if you agree to add two hours, then when you say, "Let's meet at noon," everyone in your spy network will know to meet at 10:00 a.m. Spies call this a *coefficient time code.* Of course, whenever you're dealing with times in the spy world, remember to use military time (check your *Trainee Handbook* for a refresher on this).

**2 Use a number code** Your spy network can set up a series of numbers that have special meanings. For example, some numbers could stand for locations, like 44 could mean your headquarters, while 21 could mean your locker at school. Other numbers could mean much more, like 82 could mean "Plan to meet at the usual time and place this week." Be sure to keep a secret, hidden copy of the code numbers and what they mean.

#13

# OPERATION TRUST Me

In the spy world, it's tough to know when you can trust someone. This is especially true when a spy uses a **courier** to deliver information back to headquarters. When the courier and the spy meet for the first time, how will the spy know that the person she meets is the actual courier and not a **counterspy** setting a trap? Try this operation to learn two ways a spy checks someone's **bona fides** (or good faith, honesty, and sincerity).

## Stuff You'll Need

- Scissors
- Ruler
- One sheet of green construction paper (roughly 9 x 12 inches [23 x 30 cm])

## Your Network

- Four or more friends to pose as possible couriers

## What You Do

### Part 1: The Parole

One way to check someone's bona fides is to use a special code phrase called a **parole**.

**1** Establish a parole with your friend. Paroles usually involve a question and a response. For example, if you ask, "Did you see a small dog running past here?" the correct response would be "A little brown dog?" Try to think of a question that could occur in a normal conversation with a stranger. After all, if you end up asking the question to the wrong person, you would not want to raise suspicion.

Did you see a small dog running past here?
A little brown dog?

**2** Have a friend (who'll serve as your **handler**) set up a meeting between you and another friend without telling you which friend it is. Your handler should then send several friends over to meet you. When you meet the first friend, ask your parole question. If your friend gives you the correct response, then he is the courier you're supposed to meet. If he gives you another response (like "What dog?"), then he's not the courier, and you will ask the same question to the next friend.

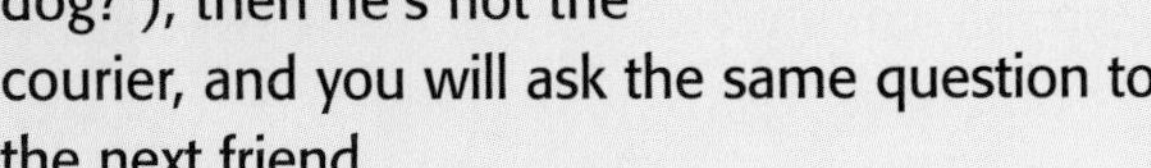

**3** When you get the correct response to your question, you'll know you've met your courier!

## Part 2: Torn Dollar Bill

Another way to check someone's bona fides is to use a torn piece of paper. Sometimes spies will use a dollar bill for this purpose, but in this case, we'll just create something that *looks* like a dollar. (We don't want to waste money!)

**1** To begin, cut the green construction paper into $2\frac{1}{2}$ x 6-inch ($6\frac{1}{2}$ x 15-cm) rectangles. (That's about the size of a dollar bill.)

**2** Next, recruit four friends and give one "dollar bill" to each person. The friends should tear their "dollars" in half.

**3** You then leave the room.

**4** Your friends should decide which of them will play the part of your courier. Once chosen, the courier should place one half of her torn "dollar" in the center of the room and the other half in her pocket.

**5** The other friends should also place one half of their "dollars" in their pockets. They should throw the other halves away.

## SPYtales

Julius and Ethel Rosenberg were members of an international spy ring that gave secrets about the American atomic bomb to the Soviet Union during the 1940s.

Julius Rosenberg was an American communist who supported the Soviet Union after it entered World War II against Germany. Soon, though, Rosenberg's support for the Soviet Union got him fired from his job in the U.S. Signal Corps (part of the army). At that time, he became a secret agent for the Soviet Union, and his wife, Ethel, helped him in his spy work. The Rosenbergs then became part of a larger **spy network** and recruited others, including Ethel's brother, David Greenglass. The spy network gave the Soviets secret information about the atomic bomb research being conducted in Los Alamos, New Mexico. The information was passed through couriers, and the Rosenbergs had a special system for checking a courier's bona fides. They would tear a Jell-o box in half, and only the real courier would have the matching half.

**6** You then reenter the room and try to find your courier. Pick up the piece of paper in the center of the room and try to match it to the other halves that your friends have in their pockets. Can you find the matching half of the paper and identify your courier correctly?

## More from Headquarters

Instead of using a torn "dollar bill," you can use a playing card to find your courier. Just tear (or cut) the card in half, keep one half, and make sure your courier has the other half. And by the way, to avoid ruining a whole deck of cards (taking one card away can do that!), try to use a deck that's already missing some cards.

## What's the Secret?

It's impossible to tear two pieces of paper in exactly the same way. Paper is made of wood fibers that have been pressed together, and the fibers are arranged in different ways and can be of various lengths. When you tear paper, the fibers come apart. Since no two pieces of paper have fibers with the same arrangement and length, all paper tears differently. Even if you tried, you could not make identical tears in two pieces of paper.

*(continued from page 23)*

At lunchtime, you get the hall pass and walk to the water fountain near the main office. You hide around a corner to try to see if anyone comes to plant a message.

A lot of students are stopping to get a drink. You lean forward to get a better view, but someone taps you on the shoulder. When you turn around, you see that it's Mr. Smith, the principal.

"Aren't you supposed to be at lunch?" he asks.

You show him the hall pass and say that you just came to get a drink, but Mr. Smith doesn't buy it.

"I've been watching you hide around the corner for the last five minutes," he says. "It's time to go back to lunch."

You do as the principal says, telling yourself that you'll return to the water fountain after school to investigate.

After class is dismissed, you rush down to the water fountain and quickly search it. Nothing unusual. You wait for a while, but no one stops by.

Whoever it was, you must've scared him or her off. There won't be a message delivery now!

■ This is a dead end. Go back and try again!

OPERATION

#14

# BLIND Code

In **Operation Call Out**, you learned how a piece of tape on a sign and a line of chalk on a curb can be **coded** signals. As with any code, the key is that the signals are meaningless to all but a choice few.

A **blind code** is another type of **call-out signal** system that uses a newspaper ad or a bulletin board posting to send a message. Does that sound too public? Then try this operation to see how public announcements can be private, too!

## Stuff You'll Need

- **Paper**
- **Pen or marker**
- **Tape or thumbtack**

## Your Network

- **Several friends to respond to your blind code**

## What You Do

**1** Meet with your **spy network** to create a fake bulletin board sign that will serve as a signal to your spy network that there will be a meeting at your house at 1600 hours (4:00 p.m.). For example, the sign could be like the one on the left. It doesn't matter what your sign says, as long as everyone in your spy network will recognize it as a signal.

**2** Arrange to have your friends look for the sign on the main bulletin board at school every day.

**3** When you want to have a meeting, stick the sign on the bulletin board. When your friends see the message, they'll know the meeting is on. If anyone else sees the sign, they'll just think someone wasn't very careful with her necklace!

## More from Headquarters

What other types of signs might be good for blind codes? Yard sales? Lost cats? Remember, you don't want your sign to attract a lot of unwanted attention.

## What's the Secret?

A blind code is called "blind" because the average reader is *blind* to it. Get it? Just make sure your bulletin board posting sounds ordinary, so it doesn't make anyone suspicious.

CLASSIFIEDS

Dodge-'71 Diplomat, needs engine work. $1000. Phone (703) 451-9780 (call next Mon., Wed., Fri., 1p.m.)

## SPYtales

This month's Spy Feature (on page 45) will tell you all about Robert Hanssen, an FBI **mole** who spied for the Russians from 1979-2001. Hanssen used a blind code system to communicate with his Russian handlers. He instructed the Russians to run a classified ad in the *Washington Times* during a certain period if they wanted to continue their discussions with him. Here's what the ad looked like (on the left).

## SPYquest

(continued from page 20)

You decide to keep thinking about it, and you say good-bye to Sarah when you pass her house. You look at the piece of stationery, trying to think of a connection between the message and the word "red."

That's when it hits you: The flowers decorating the paper are *red*! Did the sender mean that you needed your red filter to "read" the message?

You race home and when you get to your room, you take out your red filter and put it over the flowers. You're right—there's a message, and not one, but two! One of them says: YOU NEED A COMMUNICATIONS EXPERT. The other says: HISTORY P. 134.

You're not sure how the person knows about Spy Force One, but you bet that HISTORY P. 134 is the page for the grille. You take out your history textbook, turn to the page, and put the grille over it. Sure

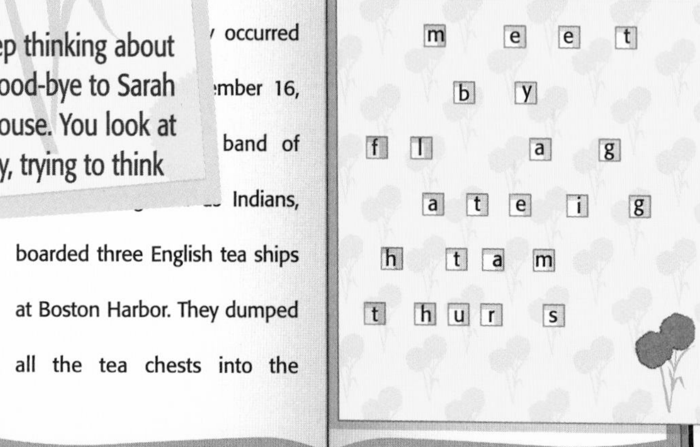
occurred
ember 16,
band of
Indians,
boarded three English tea ships
at Boston Harbor. They dumped
all the tea chests into the
m e e t
b y
f l a g
a t e i g
h t a m
t h u r s

enough, another message appears: MEET BY FLAG AT EIGHT A.M. THURS.

The next morning, you get up early and walk to school.

You see someone standing next to the flagpole who seems very familiar, and you walk up to her. You're about to ask if she's the one who's been sending you the messages, but then you realize something.

"Hey, aren't you in my history class?" you ask.

"Yeah," she says. "My name's Flora. I just moved here last month."

"How'd you find out about Spy Force One?" you ask.

"I overheard you and your friends talking about it, so I decided to send you some secret messages to prove that I've got what it takes to be a good spy. I slipped the scytale in your book when you weren't looking that morning, and everything else was pretty easy."

She pauses. "So, will you let me be in your network?"

You've got to admit that Flora was pretty good, so you call another meeting of your spy network that afternoon. Everyone agrees, and it's settled: Flora will come on board as Spy Force One's new communications expert!

So, you found out who was sending the mysterious messages *and* you got a new member in your network! Not bad!

■ Congratulations! Quest accomplished!

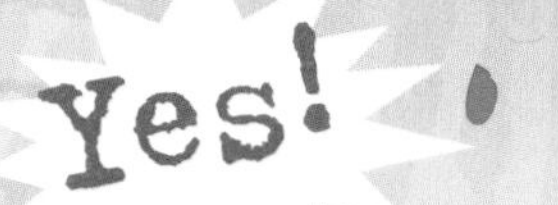
Yes!

# Robert Hanssen, FBI Mole

Robert Hanssen was an experienced **counterintelligence** officer at the FBI (Federal Bureau of Investigation). His job was to catch spies from Russia and other foreign countries. But in the end, it was Hanssen who got caught, because he led a double life. He was also a **mole** who betrayed the FBI (and his country) and spied for the Russians for more than two decades, from 1979 to 2001.

Robert Hanssen, an FBI mole from 1979 to 2001.

Hanssen sure didn't seem like a traitor. He looked like a typical suburban dad. He had a wife and six kids, and he lived in a quiet Virginia neighborhood, right outside of Washington D.C. Neighbors often saw Hanssen walking his dog at night in a neighborhood park, but he rarely stopped to chat with anyone. He seemed shy and distant. Still, however, people who knew Hanssen thought of him as a good father, a good husband, and a good professional.

Really, though, Hanssen was spying on his country, and he was in the perfect spot to do that. For twenty-five years, he rose through the ranks of the FBI's National Security Division. Unlike other FBI officers who wanted the action of working on dramatic bank robberies and fighting against organized crime, Hanssen preferred the challenge of counterintelligence, which was like piecing together a difficult puzzle.

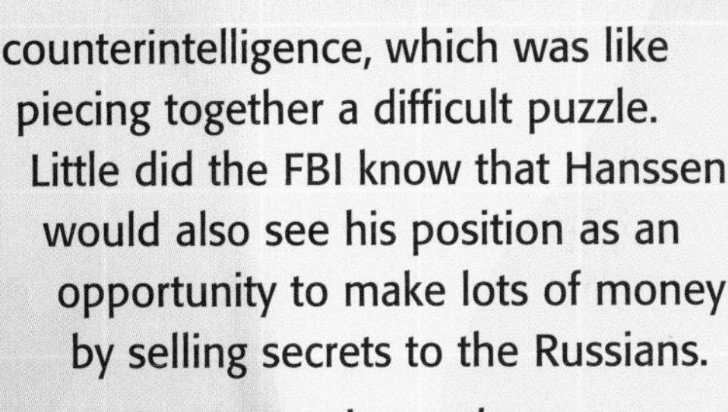

Little did the FBI know that Hanssen would also see his position as an opportunity to make lots of money by selling secrets to the Russians.

In 1979, using a phony name, Hanssen walked into a New York City office where Soviet military intelligence (GRU) officers secretly worked, and offered to sell American government secrets. To prove himself, Hanssen gave the Russians the name of one of America's most important GRU agents, Major General Dmitri Polyakov, code name TOPHAT. This act established that Hanssen would be a useful and believable spy for the Russians, and it also eliminated a GRU source who might have betrayed Hanssen back to the FBI. Hanssen did this even though he knew that Polyakov was likely to be killed (and he *was* killed a few years later).

In September of 1985, to advance his career, Hanssen accepted a promotion as a field supervisor in the FBI's New York office. Even with his increased salary, he had trouble covering the expenses of his large family, and

**Hanssen put a piece of tape on this entrance sign to Foxstone Park whenever he had placed information in Dead Drop Ellis.**

he again decided to sell secrets to the Russians. This time, however, he chose the KGB (the intelligence service of the former Soviet Union).

Over the next twenty-two years, Hanssen turned over more than two dozen computer diskettes full of classified documents—a total of roughly 6,000 pages of information! In return for this, the Russians paid Hanssen more than $600,000 in cash and diamonds, plus additional funds in a Russian bank account. The total amount Hanssen earned was roughly $1.4 million.

Here's a short list of some of Hanssen's most damaging handiwork:

- Hanssen turned over the names of nine Soviet officials who were secretly working with U.S. intelligence. Three of these men were later executed.
- Hanssen told the Russians about how the U.S. government planned to keep itself running in the event of a nuclear attack.
- He revealed to Moscow the existence of a spy tunnel beneath the Russian Embassy in Washington, D.C.
- He gave the Russians the U.S. national intelligence budget, which contained details about American counterintelligence plans.

To accomplish all this, Hannsen and his Russian handler developed a complex system to transfer information.

When Hanssen had materials to pass along, he would place a large thumbtack on a telephone pole along a well-traveled road in the Washington area. This served as a **call-out signal**. Hanssen's handler drove by the telephone pole every day, and when the thumbtack was there, the handler knew that a **dead drop** site in Foxstone Park (near Hanssen's home in Virginia) was now active and would be loaded at a pre-set time.

Hanssen would wrap his information (in the form of documents and computer disks) in a black plastic trash bag and seal it with tape to protect it from the weather. With the materials ready, Hanssen would place a piece of tape on the sign near the entrance to the park. This tape served as a drop site signal to tell his handler that the information could be picked up at Dead Drop Ellis, which was located beneath a bridge in the park. Hanssen would then tuck his plastic bag under the base of the bridge in a place that was out of sight, but still dry. A while later, Hanssen's handler would come by to pick up the information. He would remove the tape left by Hanssen as a signal that the drop had been unloaded.

**Dead Drop Ellis was located under this footbridge.**

An aerial view of Hanssen's house and Dead Drop Ellis.

Dead Drop Ellis wasn't the only drop site that Hanssen used. The FBI later received secret files from Moscow that revealed code names for several other dead drops, including one called Dead Drop Lewis, which was underneath the wooden stage of an outdoor amphitheater.

Even though Hanssen carefully followed his undercover communication procedures, he was always worried that the FBI was on to him. On more than seventy occasions, he searched the FBI's computers using key words that included his name and address to see if the FBI **counter-spies** suspected him. But he was a hard man to catch.

Although Hanssen's brother-in-law, FBI agent Mark Wauck, told his superiors in 1990 that he suspected Robert Hanssen was a spy for the Russians, they failed to investigate. Convicted FBI spy Earl Pitts also informed the FBI that he suspected Robert Hanssen was a possible spy. But it wasn't until the late 90's, when Hanssen's identity was uncovered through tips from a Russian **defector** (that is, a former Russian intelligence officer who fled to the U.S.), that the FBI set up a full-scale investigation with the CIA, the Department of State, and the Department of Justice. They began to compare Hanssen's activities to the information they'd received from the Russians. Also, when they checked a black plastic garbage bag that the Russian defector had given them, they found one of Hanssen's thumbprints. It wasn't long before the investigators confirmed that Hanssen was indeed a Russian spy.

Hanssen was finally caught in February, 2001, near Dead Drop Ellis, where he had just hidden a plastic garbage bag full of secret U.S. documents. As he was being arrested, Hanssen said to his FBI colleagues: "What took you so long?"

Hanssen pleaded guilty to spying on his country, and in order to be spared the death penalty, he agreed to cooperate with the government's investigation. He was sentenced to life in prison without the possibility of parole.

This spy case could prove to be one of the most damaging intelligence failures in American history, since Hanssen spied for so long (over a period of twenty-two years) and gave the Russians such a wide variety of important information. Because of this, the FBI has taken steps to increase its internal security. It now monitors its employees more closely and requires all officers with access to highly sensitive information to undergo lie detector tests. Still, though, to ensure that intelligence services stay free of damaging moles in the future, a new generation of sharp counterspies is needed. Who knows—maybe some of them will have started their training at Spy University!

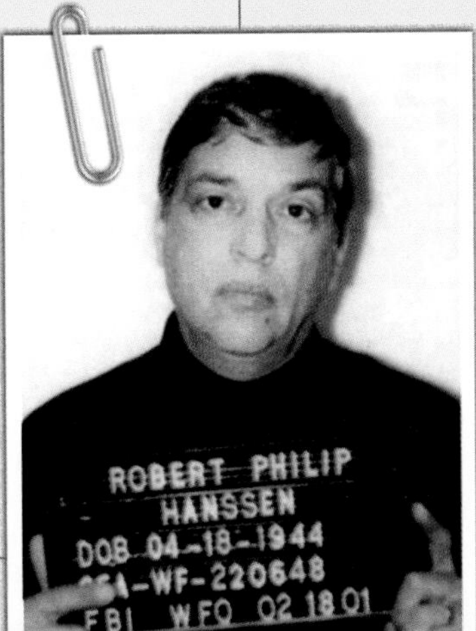


Hanssen's mug shot.

# catch you later!

You now have lots of undercover communication options, spy trainee! You've learned plenty of ways to hide your messages, and you've got a whole new set of strategies for safe and successful meetings, exchanges, and conversations with your spy network.

Here's a final message for you this month. It's a quote by a French writer from the seventeenth century named Francois Duc de la Rochefoucauld. He might not have been a spy himself, but he sure had some good advice for clever spies like you! We'll give you the start of the quote, and you can use your grille to read the rest of it (just like you did in **Operation Swiss Cheese** on page 27).

## "The Height of Cleverness Is..."

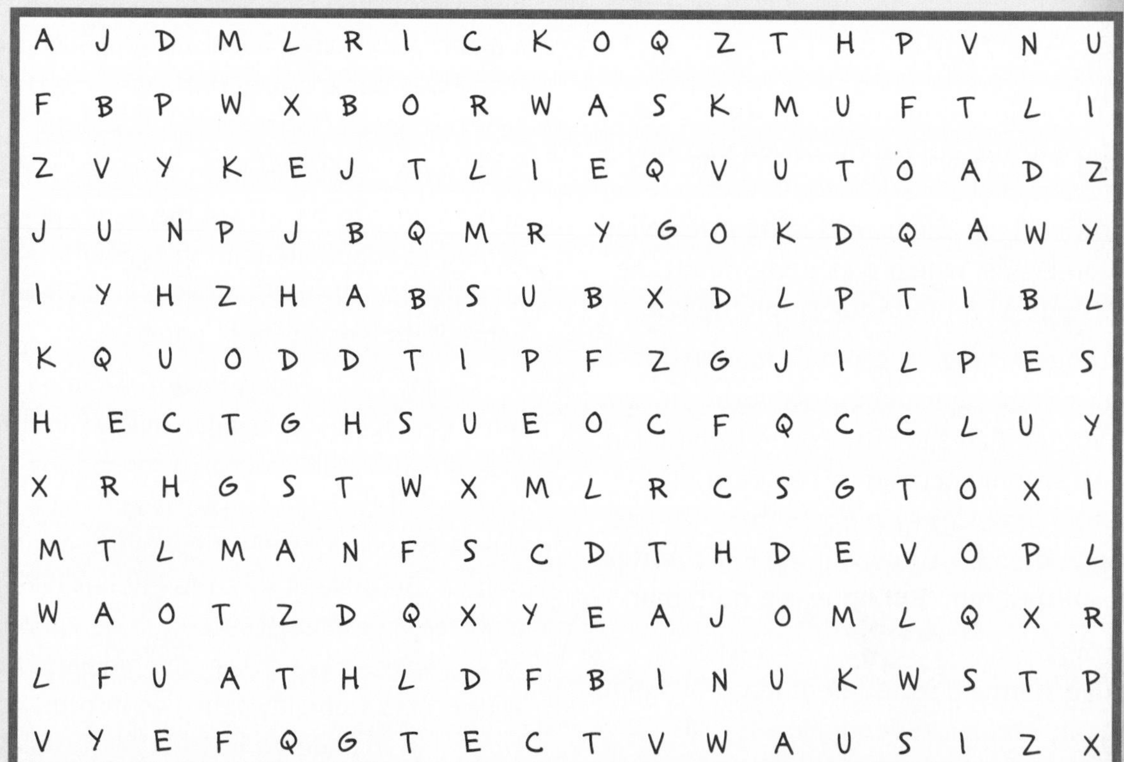

| A | J | D | M | L | R | I | C | K | O | Q | Z | T | H | P | V | N | U |
|---|---|---|---|---|---|---|---|---|---|---|---|---|---|---|---|---|---|
| F | B | P | W | X | B | O | R | W | A | S | K | M | U | F | T | L | I |
| Z | V | Y | K | E | J | T | L | I | E | Q | V | U | T | O | A | D | Z |
| J | U | N | P | J | B | Q | M | R | Y | G | O | K | D | Q | A | W | Y |
| I | Y | H | Z | H | A | B | S | U | B | X | D | L | P | T | I | B | L |
| K | Q | U | O | D | D | T | I | P | F | Z | G | J | I | L | P | E | S |
| H | E | C | T | G | H | S | U | E | O | C | F | Q | C | C | L | U | Y |
| X | R | H | G | S | T | W | X | M | L | R | C | S | G | T | O | X | I |
| M | T | L | M | A | N | F | S | C | D | T | H | D | E | V | O | P | L |
| W | A | O | T | Z | D | Q | X | Y | E | A | J | O | M | L | Q | X | R |
| L | F | U | A | T | H | L | D | F | B | I | N | U | K | W | S | T | P |
| V | Y | E | F | Q | G | T | E | C | T | V | W | A | U | S | I | Z | X |

**So, use your red filter to check your answer below, and we'll see you next month!**